To Rachel,
Always and Forever

ACKNOWLEDGMENTS

I want to start first by thanking my wife, Rachel. She is by my side at all times and her love is unwavering. Also, my parents, Paul & Linda, have given me immeasurable support. Their wisdom and encouragement have helped me through times of discouragement and they have made me who I am. I also want to thank my children, Elijah, Jason, Kyle, Kristen, Addelyen, Lilyanna, and Junior for their love. My in-laws, Gerald and Korinthia Massey, have welcomed me into their family and have always treated me as their son. For that I am always grateful.

I am indebted to my former professors Larry McDonald, James Porowski, Greg Lawson, Ken Coley, Travis Bradshaw, Larry Purcell, and John Hammett. They have invested in my life and their commitment to God's Word is unmistakable.

First Baptist Icard has made it possible for me to spend the necessary time to see this book become a reality. They have been committed to me and my family during our time as their pastor and I look forward to seeing what God is going to do with our family of faith.

Justin Smith, my friend and fellow minister, gave me invaluable feedback on the composition and flow of the study guide.

Finally, I know that I, on my own, am incapable of undertaking this work. The credit for this book goes to Christ and His longsuffering with someone like me. During these months of writing I was often reminded of Jesus' words when He said, "Apart from me you can do nothing" (Jn 15:5).

CONTENTS

1

Revival

I often lament, whether during a sermon or via social media, about the social and political decay of our nation. I read stories about teenagers who gun down a visitor to our country because they are bored. There are news clips about a war hero who is beaten to death by young men who, at sixteen, already have criminal records. I listen to reports about political impasses and ungodly agendas and I am saddened that things have gone this far. I try to lament while at the same time pointing to the solution to these stories of depravity—the Gospel of Jesus Christ.

I express my grief about the condition of our world understanding that we live as fallen human beings who have rejected the commandments and promises of our Creator. As believers in Christ, we are the redeemed children of the living God but we live among the ungodly and thus should not be surprised when they act in accordance with a fallen nature. Some, dare I say many, preachers have taken to condemning sinners to Hell long before the Savior has done so. We have abandoned these fallen creatures to their sin and unrighteousness. However, while our Redeemer has not yet turned His back on our nation or her people, we know that time is ticking away as the snowball that is history tumbles quickly out of control toward its ending point.

Our spiritual condition is not a new one. The issues that face the church in the 21st century are not unique. Rome was a pagan city that celebrated its culture of death. Medieval Europe saw debauchery of every kind. C.H. Spurgeon faced a vast sea of disbelief in the scope and authority of Scripture during the "Down-Grade Controversy" of 1887. Martyn Lloyd-Jones, in his great work *Revival*, reminds the church of this fact. Man has not changed and neither has our Creator. We need not believe we face some new problem, but rather must realize that we have the same need that every generation before has had.

What we need right now are not more or less laws, more or less government, more or less education, or more or less tolerance. Let me propose that what we need is revival—a revival in our love for God's Word. However, before a resounded "amen" is heard in response to this statement, we would do well to consider what revival is. I believe it is imperative that we do not misunderstand the thing we so often say we need. Revival is not when drunks stop drinking, drug addicts get clean, adulterers become faithful, prostitutes switch jobs, politicians retire, gays go straight, Pharisees embrace faith, Sadducees grasp the resurrection, atheists see God, agnostics know God, and Darwinists understand Genesis. These things may be good but, unfortunately this is how too many Christians define revival. It is, frankly, a shallow understanding.

In the pages that follow, I want to take a different route. I want us to journey a road less traveled. I do so out of fear that revival tarries because we start ahead of its foundation. I have read too often of what you and I should do to see revival. The actions we should take or the mindsets we should adopt become the first priority. While these are normally accurate depictions of what may very well be required to see the onset of our spiritual renaissance, I fear we start too far ahead of our actual spiritual condition. We try to build walls—the actions we should take or the mindsets we should adopt—before the foundation has been laid. We simply are not ready to experience God's revival.

I want to attempt—with full disclosure of my inabilities—to call us further back than where we are accustomed to beginning when we think about being revived. I want to call us back to the **foundation of revival—God's Word.**

Revival is when God's Word is preached, and read, and understood. Revival is when God's people fall in love with His Word. This renewal that so many believers say they want occurs when we rightly divide what God has said and embrace It as not only the guiding light of our lives, but the foundation on which our very existence as Christ followers must be built. God's Word is light in the darkness, rain in the desert, shelter for the homeless, asylum for the refugee, and hope for sinners.

The Word is God's revelation to His people. He has spoken and He calls us to listen. Al Mohler, in *Words from the Fire*, lays out a number of things that may be true if God has not spoken. None of them offer any hope for the future. However, he writes, "If God has spoken, everything has changed. If God has spoken, then the highest human aspirations must be to hear what the creator has said....If we are to know Him, He must speak—and He has!" (pp.16-18).

When God's Word falls on us, It will accomplish all that He desires for It to do. It shall succeed in the thing in which He sends It. Friends, if we try to have revival outside of God's Word, we will end up with nothing. We have nothing to be revived about. Our self-serving efforts may generate happiness. They might generate some type of manufactured, fake joy. Our church attendance might grow. However, there are plenty of churches, big and small, that do not live in God's Word. They may be well attended. People may give. People may get excited. People might even do good things. But friends, that is not revival. Revival is you and I listening to the word of God and It changing our hearts—it giving us direction and leading us to where we should go. David Dockery and David Nelson in *A Theology for the Church*, write "The purpose of Scripture is to place men and women in right standing before God and to enable believers to see God's glory in all of life's activities and efforts" (pp. 130-31). God sets His Word as the foundation for revival because It does not return empty or void.

This book will examine Isaiah 55; what I believe is a great recipe for revival. C.H. Spurgeon called this "the great chapter of gospel invitation. How free! How full! How plain and pressing are the calls to receive grace!" (p. 232). We have within this text the invitation, scope, foundation, and results of revival in God's Word. God unveils for us His beautiful plan to restore us from our hunger and darkness. He offers reviving rain and snow that satisfy and refurbish our weary souls.

In *Desiring God*, John Piper reminds us that God's Word is our weapon of choice against the daily attacks we face from the Evil One. Without it we go into battle vulnerable. It is our sword that leads us into the fight before us. So many believers suffer unnecessary heartache and frustration because they do not treasure God Word. They live outside the Word and feel inept to the task God has set before them. Their lives seem defeated and victory seems far off. It does not have to be this way. God calls us to live and love His

Word. Piper writes that if "we wear it, if it lives within us, what mighty warriors we can be!" (p. 151).

We wake up each morning in desperate need of revival. Praise God, He has given us His Word and It holds the key. My hope is that you grab hold of His Word. Devour It as you would the finest meal. Savor It as you would an expensive dessert. Let It consume you—all of your heart and all of your soul, and all of your strength, and all of your mind. Let's fall in love with God's reviving Word

2

The Invitation

"Come, everyone who thirsts,
come to the waters;
and he who has no money,
come, buy and eat!
Come, buy wine and milk
without money and without price.
Why do you spend your money for that which is not bread,
and your labor for that which does not satisfy?
Listen diligently to me, and eat what is good,
and delight yourselves in rich food.
Incline your ear, and come to me;
hear, that your soul may live;
and I will make with you an everlasting covenant,
my steadfast, sure love for David.
Isaiah 55:1-3

Isaiah 55 is positioned as follow up to one of my favorite passages in the Bible, Isaiah 52:13-53:12. Isaiah 52 and 53 provide such a beautiful picture of the coming Messiah. I get chills every time I read it and think about Isaiah's picture of the suffering and triumph of Christ. I know it is no coincidence that the portrait of the Suffering Servant leads to the refreshing of the unstoppable word. His suffering and sacrifice make possible the refreshing of our hearts.

I want to propose to you that this text, Isaiah 55, is a wonderful recipe for revival. It is a wonderful recipe for us because it is not a twelve-step plan by which we can follow and somehow generate man-made interest in things that are not of God. It is a recipe for revival because it centers on God and His riches toward his people. His Word is at the heart of our spiritual renaissance.

This should give us hope because it shows us that we are incapable on our own of bringing forth the blessing and the joy and the gracious gifts of God. I, for one, am really glad that Isaiah makes that point because we do a really lousy job of making those things happen.

Come

He begins by presenting God's invitation to revival—an invitation to be revived by God. He says *come, everyone who is thirsty*. What a wonderful invitation because it includes everyone. Everyone has been thirsty. The richest of the rich have been thirsty. The poorest of poor have been thirsty. Young and old, tall and short, everyone!

When I first read these verses, I did so with great cheer. Regardless of whatever situation in life I have found myself, I have always been part of the "everyone." He says come, everyone who is thirsty—come to the waters. He invites them in from their thirst to a place and a position where the palate is satisfied.

He further says, *he who has no money, come, buy and eat.* That is something you will not hear at McDonalds. There is no sign at the local mom and pop's restaurant that offers this gift. Somehow, through the power of Christ, we are able to buy what we could not afford. We are able to have a cessation to our hunger though we do not have the means to purchase the catalyst of our fulfillment. Those words from Isaiah 52 and 53 ring loudly once again:

> *But he was pierced for our transgressions; he was crushed for our iniquities; upon him was the chastisement that brought us peace, and with his wounds we are healed. All we like sheep have gone astray; we have turned—every one—to his own way; and the LORD has laid on him the iniquity of us all.* (Isa 53:5-6)

We eat and drink—we are sustained—through Christ. God reminds us of this by inviting His people to be revived. Basically God is saying, "You have nothing that I want—

nothing that I need, but come! You've got no money, but come and buy."

He doesn't stop there. He says without money and without price. He says not only is there nothing you can offer, but there is nothing that you have that would matter. There is nothing that you could give that would have any benefit. If you had all the money in the world, the thing that God is offering you would still be too valuable for you to buy. John Calvin, in his commentary on Isaiah, writes, "He shews that we are poor and utterly destitute, and that we have nothing by which we can become entitled to God's favour; but that he kindly invites us, in order that he may freely bestow everything without any recompense" (p. 157). The richest person who has ever lived could not exchange all of his riches for a moment of God's blessing. Yet even with nothing to offer he says four times in verse one, *come.*

Stale Bread

He asks a question in verse two, *why do you spend your money for that which is not bread and your labor for that which does not satisfy?* Why is it that we so often try to manufacture God's work? Why do we try to manipulate the Holy Spirit's movements? We try to make something happen. When we have events at the church I pastor, we make really nice signs and we put them up throughout the community. However, that does not make people come. Trust me; I have made really nice signs for really bad events.

It does not matter if members of my church invite someone a thousand times or I give a million well-crafted post-sermon invitations, God has to be at work for a life to be changed. Some time back, the church I pastor hosted a weekend conference on spiritual revival that served as foundational for me in writing this book. Though the sole purpose of this weekend was spiritual awakening, we had to go into the weekend knowing that just because we had this event there was no promise that God would send us revival. If we think an event will cause revival to happen or if we think that our increased church attendance will cause God to send His blessings, we are sadly mistaken.

God calls us to come—come with nothing—come with no presuppositions; come empty handed! Come and drink. We, however, often go in a different direction. We labor for things that do not matter—the things that do not satisfy. We invest our time and effort doing much that is frivolous. God, meanwhile, is disappointed in our attempts that are irrelevant and quickly fade away. They are a waste.

Think of it like this. I have a wonderful couple in my church that from time to time will bake my family fresh bread. This bread is pretty fantastic and is far superior to anything I buy at the store. Plus, on top of that, it is free! How ridiculous would it be for me, while having this fresh bread on my table, to go and spend money on inferior bread—bread that compared to what I have been given is stale and moldy. I am not the most conscientious shopper, but I know my food.

Our typical mindset toward the things of God is no different. We have a free gift but we go into a store and spend our money on moldy, stale bread. Surely this inferior bread is something we would never eat. Yet we not only eat it with gladness, but serve it on our dinner table for friends and family to eat. Why would we do such a disturbing thing?

God wants to replace this stale bread—these ill-fated endeavors and our idolatrous materialism—with something different. Jesus said:

> *Do not labor for food that perishes, but for the food that endures to external life, which the Son of Man will give you....I am the bread of life; whoever comes to me shall not hunger and whoever believes in me shall never thirst.* (Jn 6:27, 35)

The Bread and Fountain

Arthur Pink in *Spiritual Growth* writes that, "nothing but a knowledge of God can satisfy the spirit of man, as naught but His love can content his soul" (p. 40-41). God aids His children in understanding this fact and attracts their hearts to Himself. As God works in the heart, the sinner is able to more clearly see how he has been deceived by sin. From there he can see how sin "has deluded him into vainly imagining that the things of time and sense could afford him satisfaction, until he discovers…he has 'spent money for that which is not bread' and 'labored for that which satisfith not'" (p. 41). God calls us to something different. He calls us to eat what is good. As Pink reminds us: "until God becomes our 'Portion' the soul is left with an aching void" (p. 41).

The good news is that One who is the Bread and the Fountain calls them to listen. He has something to say. Their efforts are in vain but His words allow them to *eat what is good*. They are able to *delight* themselves *in rich food*. Desperation, due to their lack of resources, had caused them to lean on themselves, but the voice of God cries out for them to listen and incline their ears and hear.

God is offering them what they could not buy. He is offering them the ability to come into a relationship with Him—an everlasting covenant. They are able to hear His Word and consume it. Elsewhere in Scripture, we see that the Word is to be eaten (Ez 3:1-3), to be devoured, and to satisfy. The Christ follower is not to worry about all the other things going on—not to worry about the world around and the chaos around us but to eat the bread that never leaves the stomach empty. God says there is life found in listening to and coming to Him. This is life far beyond bread. This is a covenant that stretches far beyond the quenching of thirst.

In Mark 9:2-13, we have the amazing account of the Transfiguration. Jesus takes Peter, James, and John up on a high mountain. Jesus is transfigured before them and His clothes become radiant and brilliantly white. Suddenly, Moses and Elijah appear with Jesus! Moses, the Law giver, and Elijah, the great prophet, are talking with Jesus. This leaves the disciples dumbfounded and terrified. God, speaking out of Heaven, says, *this is my beloved Son; listen to him* (Mk 9:7). With everything that could be said in the moment, God says that those present should listen to His Son. The giver of the law is present and the great prophet of the Old Testament is there, but we are told to listen to the Words of the Son of God.

Here is the first step to revival. God has given an invitation to listen to what He has said. It seems simple. It seems easy. However, we get caught up in trying to do everything else. We try to manufacture revival and renewal through our efforts. Doing so always ends in disappointment. Our hearts sink low when we can't make God do the thing we desire and yet He still cries out is *listen to me.*

From the invitation in vv.1-3, Isaiah's message moves to the scope of revival in vv. 4-9 and that will be where our journey resumes in chapter three.

3

The Scope

Behold, I made him a witness to the peoples,
a leader and commander for the peoples.
Behold, you shall call a nation that you do not know,
and a nation that did not know you shall run to you,
because of the LORD your God, and of the Holy One of
Israel,
for he has glorified you.
"Seek the LORD while he may be found;
call upon him while he is near;
let the wicked forsake his way,
and the unrighteous man his thoughts;
let him return to the LORD, that he may have compassion on
him,
and to our God, for he will abundantly pardon.
For my thoughts are not your thoughts,
neither are your ways my ways, declares the LORD.

For as the heavens are higher than the earth,
so are my ways higher than your ways
and my thoughts than your thoughts.

Isaiah 55:4-9

Television is an interesting medium for communication. It, like most other communication tools, has been used for both good and bad. I remember being told as a child that too much television would rot my brain out. The jury is still out on that one. At any moment you can watch infomercials, SpongeBob SquarePants, the National Football League or a previously recorded Billy Graham Crusade. Interestingly enough, depending on the makeup of a particular household, all of that programing may be running on separate televisions at the same time.

Television allows us to see the wide spectrum of the human existence. A reality show or entertainment news program may reveal the excesses of the celebrity lifestyle while also containing a commercial featuring those same celebrities asking for help in feeding the starving children of the world. You can literally see it all on television.

Right or wrong, there is a huge spectrum in the life experiences people have. Some are born to riches while others earn it through toil and heartache. Some live but a short while, starving to death simply because of the location of their birth. Some live joyous lives filled with excitement and contentment. Others never know happiness, living and dying in obscurity. This is reality and though many have tried, they have been hard pressed to change it. Regardless of their situation in life, most people do not lead revived existences. Most people have not accepted God's invitation to be renewed and filled through the free offering of God's invitation that we explored in the previous chapter.

I want to propose to you in the chapter before us that falling in love with the precious Word of God is, in part, about falling in love with the scope of His revival. What I mean by this is that we must begin seeing the world as God sees it. Our wonderful and merciful savior has given us this great invitation to be revived in His word. As we dig into it, soaking it in, and embracing its renewal, we will begin to see things as God does—we will have the mind of Christ (Rom 12:2; Phil 2:5). We lead small, meaningless lives, or at least that is what we believe. God is really big. He has big plans for His people to lead big, important lives.

The question then becomes, what does God desire? His invitation in the first verses of this passage was to come and eat. Those who are rich and those who are poor. Those who have and those who have not. I have heard people say that God wants to revive this church or that. I have even heard about God's desire to revive our nation. While God does revive us, revive our churches, and revive our communities, I want to purpose to you that those do not even come close to the full desires of God's heart. His Word is powerful and the scope of His revival extends all over His creation.

All Nations

In verse five we read *behold you shall call a nation that you do not know, and a nation that did not know you shall run to you because of the Lord your God and of the Holy One of Israel, for He has gloried you.* For Israel, much of their salvation was tied up in the land that God had given them. Their focus was on a strip of dirt. If that land was not important, they would not still be fighting nearly 3,000 years after Isaiah penned these words, but they do. Each and every day people are killed over this strip of land. In contrast to the clamor for land, Isaiah shares that the scope of God's revival and renewal is going to be so much greater than just the land they see around them. It is going to be so much greater than just the strip of land they live on and the people who lay claim to that land. John Calvin writes that God, "intends to explain…that the church shall be collected out of various peoples so that they who were formerly scattered shall be gathered into one body; for the word 'run' relates to harmony of faith…although by nature the knowledge of God is engravened on the hearts of all men, yet it is so confused and dark, and entangled by man's errors, that, if the light of the world be not added to it, by knowing they know not God, but wander miserably in darkness" (pp. 163-64).

That God's renewal is for all nations is made clear in multiple Scripture passages. Abraham is told that his offspring shall bless all the nations (Gn 22:18). Jesus says in Matthew's Gospel that, "This gospel of the kingdom will be proclaimed throughout the whole world as a testimony to all nations, and then the end will come (Mt 24:14). In John's vision recorded in the book of Revelation, he hears a new song, sung in praise to the Lamb: "Worthy are You to take the book and to break its seals; for You were slain, and purchased for God with Your blood men from every tribe and tongue and people and nation" (Rv 5:9). Two chapters later he sees "a great multitude that no one could number, from every nation, from all tribes and peoples and languages, standing before the throne and before the Lamb, clothed in white robes, with palm branches in their hands" (Rv 7:9). Throughout the biblical storyline, God seeks out the nations for salvation. God's scope is big.

Daniel Akin, in *Five Who Changed the World*, tells of the great missionary to the nations Jim Elliot. Elliot was martyred for his unwavering faith in Christ. Because Elliot desired that the nations would enjoy their creator, Akin writes, "The nations must hear that this God reigns, He rules sovereignly over the whole world....He's got the whole world in His hands" (p. 92).

God's desire for the salvation of the nations is the reason, for instance, the denomination I belong to, the Southern Baptist Convention, puts a heavy emphasis on missions to people all over the world. We want to reach those who do not know Christ. We do this because God is working in the hearts and lives of people in all nations. He wants to send revival to all people. He wants to renew all people.

If we think about revival in the small scope of our own hearts, we miss what God is doing. It should revive us when we look across the nations and see our brothers and sisters both standing for their faith and dying for their faith. Our hearts should be pricked when we see what God is doing in their lives. God is at work in every corner of the world. The places that appear to be the darkest and furthest from the reach of His Word are exactly where His revival will take place.

If you want to see revival, go and look at what God is doing through His people in some of the darkest places on earth. These are the places where God is moving; the Church is expanding even as people are suffering for their faith. Why is this? Because God is offering His revival to all nations.

We would be hard-pressed to proclaim our love for God's word without a desire to see the nations revived. It is a pitiful spiritual condition that many in our world live in.

Too many have embraced false gods that do not save. The responsibility for that condition falls on Christians who have yet to fall deeply enough in love with the Word of God to do something about it. The nations cry out for salvation and God's Word compels us, "go"!

All Sinners

Next, in vv. 6-7, we see that the scope of revival is to all sinners. Not only is God's revival to all nations, but He wants to save all sinners. His revival is not reserved for those who seem to have it all together. He does not simply desire to revive those who have crafted out a pretty good morality. Jesus spent His incarnate time with the lowest in His society. He spent time with those most affected by sin—those with whom sin had dealt harshly. He did so because God makes available revival and renewal to all sinners.

In my experience, there seems to be three types of popular preaching and thought when it comes to sinners. On one end of the spectrum is the deemphasizing of sin. This vein of thought seeks to minimize the reality and consequences of sin. At its core is a humanist theology that sees an essential goodness in humanity and rejects any type of judgment, righteous wrath, or propitiatory sacrifice. This is obviously wrong. Scripture is clear that God hates sin (Prv 6:16-19; Jer 50:31). The Lord also commands those who love Him to hate evil (Ps 8:13, 97:10; Am 5:15; Rm 12:9). None are above evil and all have sinned against God

(Rm 3:23). The Apostle Paul is clear that the consequences of that sin is death (Rm 6:23). Minimizing sin is of no spiritual benefit and only serves the fleshly desires of ear-tickling preachers and guilt-ridden listeners.

There is also what I will call "sin preaching." This is marked by an abnormal obsession with sin that results in the minimization of both God's grace and His persistence in saving sinners. This type of thought provides no hope for sinners and takes great joy in their death and destruction (Ez 18:23). This line of thinking leaves out the second part of the aforementioned Romans 6:23: "but the free gift of God is eternal life in Christ Jesus our Lord." Sin preaching forgets that God sent His Son to save the world (Jn 3:16). In *A Call to Spiritual Reformation,* D.A. Carson writes about this tragic position too many Christians are in where they only enjoy bad news. Stories of illicit sin will peak their interest. They will not celebrate when the Spirit of God moves. In fact, that will ruin their interest. But let sin creep in the door and they are ready to enjoy the show (pp.84-85).

Probably the greatest irony of this hopeless outlook is the fact that its adherents claim to have been saved by, saved to, and saved from the same God they now proclaim offers only judgment. They too were sinners who needed salvation by His amazing grace and though they see themselves now under grace they cannot imagine that anyone else will get there.

To be clear, God is obsessed with sin. He hates it completely and in every situation. It is never okay and can never be justified. There will be no excuse that will suffice (Rm 1: 20). In fact, we do not fully understand ourselves and the rest of humanity outside of understanding the seriousness of sin. Consider this, R. Stanton Norman writes, "a biblical understanding of sin mandates that we assess human nature in light of the Fall and its effects (p. 475).

However, the biblical storyline tells of a persistent Savior. Day and night He is seeking His bride. He never gives up and is never deterred. He is a "God merciful and gracious, slow to anger, and abounding in steadfast love and faithfulness" (Ex 34:6, Nm 14:8; Ne 9:17; Ps 86:5, 16; 103:8; 145:8). The passage before us demonstrates this clearly: *Seek the LORD while he may be found; call upon him while he is near; let the wicked forsake his way, and the unrighteous man his thoughts; let him return to the LORD, that he may have compassion on him, and to our God, for he will abundantly pardon.*

That is a message of hope! No matter how far someone has gone—no matter how deeply they have fallen into sin— our God abundantly pardons. Think of it this way, if someone is sitting on death row, having committed the most egregious crimes, our God will abundantly pardon. They need but to call upon His name. It worries me how often I hear messages that contain no hope for sinners. Friends our nation and our society are in bad shape. However, we are not beyond the reach of our Creator. He has offered forgiveness for all of those who will come to Him. Francis Schaeffer, in *He is There and He is Not Silent,* laments that "evangelicals have made a horrible mistake by often equating the fact that man is lost and under God's judgment with the idea that man is nothing—a zero" (p.3).

This is the third and proper method of explaining God's relationship with His fallen creation. This tension (God's hatred of sin and love for His creation) in God's character must be clear for us to understand God and fall madly in love with His Word. Sin is a very real thing and human beings are extremely sinful—so sinful in fact that we have no ability to find God or be righteous. However, we have been created by a very real God who is completely just. He deals harshly with sin. He cuts no corners and makes no exceptions.

Simultaneously, He is full of grace and mercy. Not by overlooking sin, but by confronting it head on. He so loves that in spite of our seemingly infinite capacity and desire to disobey, He sent His truly infinite Son to take on sin's infinite penalty—a penalty reduced from infinite to obsolete by His propitiatory sacrifice. Jonathan Edwards wrote, "God may through Christ pardon the greatest sinner without any prejudice to the honor of His majesty. The honor of the divine majesty indeed requires satisfaction; but the sufferings of Christ fully repair the injury" (p. 269). If we miss either side of this coin of God's character, we render God's message worthless.

The fact is, sin and the Bible are at odds with one another. As Richard Owen Roberts writes in *Repentance*, "the place that the Holy Bible occupies in a society is a major factor in this rise and fall of sin. Those who are familiar with the Bible know that it speaks frequently of sin. Indeed, the Bible is the greatest single source of vital information on the subject of sin to be found anywhere in the world" (p. 15).

When we love our sin, we have a dim view of the Scriptures. We want to dismiss them or sugarcoat the parts that make us uncomfortable. God has never been in the sugarcoating business. He speaks to us clearly about the destructive reality of sin. The Bible paints a dim view of the future of sin while proposing that there is eternal hope for sinners. Unfortunately, the secular worldview that many cling to holds most sin as good and offers no promise of hope past the temporary and carnal joy of sin. To the contrary, the Word offers a cure for sin, a genuine joy, and an eternal hope.

Our God's grace is so good, so big, so wide, and so deep that there is no one in this world outside of God's loving reach. There is no one who has strayed so far that they cannot be brought back through the message of the Gospel. If we want to have revival, if we want our hearts changed by Christ's message, we will realize that God is looking to save sinners. And not just the sinners that we can clean up easily, but the sinners in whom God has to work a great miracle. The scope is all nations, the scope is all sinners.

Not Ours

The scope is big; much more expansive than I thought before I first interacted with Isaiah 55. If it were my scope, I would struggle to see past myself. I am often made keenly aware of my inept spiritual condition. I understand that it will take a lifetime of godly correction and outpourings of His blessings to even begin reflecting the Father. However, God's scope is not ours and I am so thankful for this.

I have heard way too many sermons where a confident preacher stands up and declares that there is no hope. There is no chance that God is going to move. There is no possibility that He is going to heal our nation. To them, there appears to be no situation where He will save our neighbors. It is easy to come away feeling like it is over—we have lost! I wonder if those preachers have ever turned to the end of the Book. This is one of those times where you can skip ahead and find out what happens at the end. We win! Jesus comes back and we are victorious in Him! So why would we assume that the game is over and we are defeated? That we have no hope? It is easy to do when we do not comprehend the scope of God's revival.

In vv. 8-9, He says, *My thoughts are not your thoughts*. When I contrast this verse of Scripture and my own heart, that fact is painfully easy to see. He makes the difference in my heart and His way is clear in light of His desire to renew all nations and all sinners. You and I would not have that view. I realize that everyone's heart is touched by pictures of starving children or the need for the cure to horrific diseases such as AIDS, malaria, or cancer. However, our innate heartache seems to only last until the next commercial appears on the television screen. Our lives are busy, our foreknowledge is limited, and our capacity to love is tainted by sin's curse. We do well to make it through a week taking care of ourselves and those we are responsible for. For me this remains true though I have been saved by Christ.

It is hard for me to love the nations and to love sinners. Think how difficult it is for our heart to forgive and love those who need it most. Think how hard it is to love and forgive those close to us. So it is easy for God to say "Your ways are not my ways and your thoughts are not my thoughts" because He does with ease what we can only do with a war on our intrinsic desires. His very nature is to love the unlovable.

We have to look no further than God's plan of redemption to see this made clear. You and I would go about it a different way. You and I would choose a different path. We would not give *our* son to die for the world. I know *I* would not have made that sacrifice. Maybe, just maybe, we would say we would when we look at the people around us who we love, but what about the people who are far off? What of the people we hate? There is no way we would say that we would give our son to die in their place. In spite of that, I am thankful that God said **your ways are not my mine and my thoughts are not yours.** We are not the same. In verse nine He goes further, saying, **for as the heavens are higher than the earth so are my ways higher than your ways. And my thoughts higher than your thoughts.** God sees much further than we do. He is omniscient, He understands much more than we do. He knows what is going to happen. He has seen it. He has been there. He is crafting out His will and His plan for the world. He is making it happen each and every day.

It Is Big

The more I see how big the plan that Christ has is, the more I fall in love with His Word. The more I fall in love with His Word, the more I see how expansive His work is. If we fail to listen to His message and see the scope of His work, we will treat his work like a mom and pop's diner beside some busy highway. The food is good and the service is friendly, but the reach is limited. When we fall in love with God's Word we realize that this is no small thing that we are a part of. His reach is far and wide. He is at work on every corner and in every nation. He is radically changing hearts and lives everywhere and we are called to jump in and help. Isaiah describes the incredible breadth of this work as we finish this chapter with his words:

> *The government shall be upon his shoulder,*
> *and his name shall be called*
> *Wonderful Counselor, Mighty God,*
> *Everlasting Father, Prince of Peace.*
> *Of the increase of his government and of peace there will be no*
> *end,*
> *on the throne of David and over his kingdom,*
> *to establish it and to uphold it*
> *with justice and with righteousness*
> *from this time forth and forevermore.*
> *The zeal of the LORD of hosts will do this.*
> Isaiah 9:6-7

4

The Foundation

*For as the rain and the snow come down from heaven
and do not return there but water the earth,
making it bring forth and sprout,
giving seed to the sower and bread to the eater,
so shall my word be that goes out from my mouth;
it shall not return to me empty,
but it shall accomplish that which I purpose,
and shall succeed in the thing for which I sent it.*
Isaiah 55: 10-11

I have lived my entire life in the foothills of North Carolina. Though I have traveled to a number of other places, my home is my favorite place to be. The scenery is beautiful and the climate is pretty great. It seems like the temperature is almost always in a tolerable range. The one thing I do wish was different about the foothills is our lack of snowfall. Not too far to my west, the Appalachian

Mountains receive ample snowfall each year. Very often, the piedmont region to my east does as well. However, the snow seems to leap right over the foothills leaving us with clear roads and disappointed children hoping for a day free of school.

Snowfall, at least for those of us who do not see it very often, is an awe-inspiring sight. In minutes, a little bit of snow can turn a dreary winter day into the picturesque front of a postcard. Even now, when I am most definitely beyond my sledding years, I get excited about the possibility of a snowfall. I know my kids will be excited and there will be no shortage of fun at our house.

Speaking through Isaiah in verse 10, God talks about snow, using it as an example of His revival. He invites us to be revived. He lays out how big it is, and now He shows us its foundation. God says that rain and snow come down and water the earth and do not return there. This reminds me of all those drawings of the water cycle from elementary school science books—clouds forming over the ocean and rolling in over the land. This section combines elements of the water cycle with the food chain. The water causes plants to grow, giving seed to the sower and bread to the eater. The food chain was always something I was glad to be at the top of. Without these two God-designed cycles, life could not exist. His prefect plan provides us exactly what we need.

For us to understand what He means in verse 11, we have to grapple with the implications of verse 10. The title of this book comes from verse 11, but it loses much of its meaning outside of the context of the rain and snow!

God sends precipitation. I know that is not a shocking statement, but to me it is profound. With all the available technology and twenty-four-hour networks devoted to the weather, we still have no control. If we did, we would most likely not allow the types of weather events that kill people and destroy lives. Even humanity's ability (or lack thereof) to accurately predict the weather has led to many a meteorologist being severely despised by people who were unaware of their need for an umbrella.

The precipitation of God's Word does the same thing. He sends it freely and outside of our control. I would even argue that it often comes in spite of our attempts to control or prevent it. Just like the rain and snow, it causes everything to grow. It blankets everything and changes how we see the world. I love the line from the old hymn by Elvina Hall, "sin had left a crimson stain, He washed it white as snow." What a powerful word! The Word washes over everything; even down to our sinful nature. When the rain and snow cover the earth, it cannot help but sprout.

I am always amazed at what will grow and where. I have this bale of hay outside my house. It is a leftover decoration from Halloween. I passed it the other day and there were these little green sprouts bursting out of the top. How amazing! I didn't plant them but they are there. Go search on the Internet for pictures of new growth after a forest fire. It is incredible what the rain and snow do to even the most scorched of earth. God takes the scorched earth of our lives, devastated by sin and disobedience, and sends the renewal of His rain. When He does, all things are made new.

Sustenance

When I was younger, some of my buddies and I enjoyed playing video games together. This was long before you could play with other people online; you actually had to be together, in the same room. The game I most loved playing with my friends was called *Gauntlet Legends*. The game consisted of four characters working together on a quest against evil. As your character encountered attacks from the menacing hordes, the meter that measured your health would be in a steady decline. At some point, it would be necessary to restore your health so that the quest could continue. Throughout the game we could find both bushels of fruit and chunks of meat that provided restoration to our waning health. We became so enamored with this game that we would actually strategize about who would pick up the food and when so that we could continue through the game. When our characters were nourished, they could continue on their journey. If we neglected to find sustenance, we would find ourselves starting the journey over.

Our lives need sustenance and Isaiah shares with us the nourishing effect of God's Word. All this blanketing snow and sprouting foliage has amazing consequences. There is seed for the sower and bread for the eater. God's precipitation provides for the needs of His creation. This provision is all encompassing; from the farmer who plants his crops to the final results—bread for the hungry. God's design is so incredible. The very crops the farmer grows produce more seeds which he is able to harvest, plant, and care for. Then process starts once again. God provides from beginning to end. If He is absent at any point, then everything falls apart.

This is why His Word is the foundation of our renewal. It must be our sustaining power and guide. There are a lot of actions and positions we can take that may be essential to revival and renewal, but how is it that the Christian even knows to do these things without the Word? How does the Christian know to pray or evangelize? Maybe even more fundamental: How do we know of our creator, His Son, and our need for a savior? Outside of His Word, there is no trustworthy means to gain knowledge of Christ and His Kingdom. The Bible provides us God's story from beginning to end. It shows us His conquering plan of redemption and is the blueprint for the Christian life.

Void

When you watch commercials or read advertisements that describe some type of contest or giveaway, there is almost always a disclaimer at the bottom that reads: "No purchase necessary, void where prohibited." While the "no purchase necessary" part is to be in compliance with the Federal Communications Commission, the "void" line always strikes me as odd. There are actually places that prohibit these contests that give stuff away. Some places require a pile of paperwork and fees, while others just ban them completely.

When a company wants to give things away, they have to be careful to be compliant with applicable law. Sometime this means that their offer has to be void in certain places to be valid in others. Some people simply get left out.

The promise of God's Word is that It will not return void. There is no place where it can be prohibited. Do not misunderstand, there are places that have tried, but they have and will continue to fail. There are tyrants who have sought to extinguish the Word, but they now occupy graves while the Word endures.

Just as God paints a picture of the water cycle, He now shows that His Word functions much like that cycle. It falls from His mouth and comes full circle. It plants, waters, grows, and gathers the harvest (1 Cor 3:6).

Accomplish

I am mechanically challenged. My car repair abilities are limited to calling my dad to see if he is available to help. I am also industrially challenged. If you want something built, you do not call me. I have, however, become really good at holding a flashlight or retrieving a desired tool. So in those rare moments when I build something sturdy or successfully repair a car, I am pretty proud of myself. Of course, this pride is misplaced. The reality is I've accomplished very little.

God's Word is the complete opposite. His Word accomplishes a lot. He spoke and brought everything into existence. His Word promised God's people would be a great nation. His Word demanded His people be released from captivity. His Word promised an everlasting Kingdom to a Middle Eastern king. The Word of God revealed to future-seeing men that a Savoir would be born. The Word promised an eternal kingdom, called on a religious man to be born again, and comforted a dying thief with a soon-coming paradise. The Word promised all these things and makes good on those promises. Whatever God's Word sets out to do, It accomplishes.

Succeed

I fear we are at the point in both our churches and personal lives where we label some pretty poor results as success. I believe this leaves us with a constant expectation of the mediocre. We settle for the inferior and are therefore normally uninspired. We do not strive to do more or better because we cannot imagine more than what we experience.

Falling in love with God's Word leads you to detest the mediocre. God has redeemed His creation from sin. That is something be to labeled a success! He calls people from every tribe, tongue, and nation. We are guilty of patting ourselves on the back for coming to three out of four church services in a month. If you are an alleged "super Christian," you make it to all four and contribute to the offering. When you step back and reflect on those standards, in light of what God seeks to accomplish, it really does not add up to success.

Falling in love with God's Word leads us to seek after godly success. Do not be afraid to succeed. Do not be afraid to radically alter what you are doing so it better conforms to the calling of His Word. We are the sons and daughters of God and we are called to greatness.

Revived for a Purpose

All of this is not random. It does not happen by chance—God does not just get lucky. He has a purpose in everything He does. Just as the rain and snow are indispensable, so is His Word. Nothing is accomplished without it. No real success can be realized apart from It. If we are in love with Jesus and His Word, we will live in His purpose. The writer of Hebrews hones in on this concept as he writes: "for whoever has entered God's rest has also rested from his works as God did from his" (Heb 4:10). In Christ, we do not operate with our own agendas and desires. We must put aside our own sinful initiatives and take up the mind of Christ.

God stands ready to move hearts and change lives with the power of His Word. He has made us an intrinsic part of His work. He did not save us and revive our dead lives so that we could sit idly by and continue to look dead. In fact, if we return to that same section in the book of Hebrews we find, "let us fear lest any of you should *seem* to have failed to reach it" (Heb 4:1, emphasis mine). There should be no appearance that we have not entered the rest of God. Our revival should be evident because God has purposed us for a public faith.

5

The Results

For you shall go out in joy
and be led forth in peace;
the mountains and the hills before you
shall break forth into singing,
and all the trees of the field shall clap their hands.
Instead of the thorn shall come up the cypress;
instead of the brier shall come up the myrtle;
and it shall make a name for the LORD,
an everlasting sign that shall not be cut off."
Isa 55:12-13

When I read these verses, I see a picture out of a Disney movie. There is often a personification of inanimate objects such as a tree or a tea pot. Somehow, I guess because there are really no rules in animation, they begin to sing and to dance, especially in the older, classic Disney movies. Think of *Beauty and the Beast* (I can because I have three daughters). There are items from all over the mansion that the main characters are trapped in that begin to sing and dance. There is great excitement as these magical worlds come to life. For children, this is a wonderful thing to witness as they see these items sing and dance with joy and happiness.

These big musical numbers often play out at the end of the movie. Maybe the main characters have been reunited in love or perhaps the hero has conquered the evil villain. He has defeated his foe once and for all. He has saved the land and won his princess' heart. Everyone can sing and shout with joy because evil is gone. It is not unusual for the main character and his victory over evil to win over the heart of the villain. The villain himself has had his hard heart melted away.

This is evident in the Dr. Sessus story, *How the Grinch Stole Christmas*. The Grinch, who detested Christmas and impersonated Santa, stole the toys from all the children of Whoville. The children awake and come outside on Christmas day but not as the Grinch had hoped. The Grinch had envisioned an awful scene where terrified children would awaken to have no presents and he would be victorious. Instead he hears them singing. They walk out of their houses, all the Whos of Whoville, and they begin to sing about the joy that they have in spite of the Grinch's attempt to steal Christmas. The result is a radical change of heart. The Grinch, our villain who has attempted to ruin Christmas, has his heart changed. He returns the gifts. He returns town with a warm welcome from people who are excited by the knowledge that Christmas was not about the toys that they were to receive from Santa Clause.

That is what I see here in verse 12. I see a vision of hearts being changed by the powerful Word of God. They have been changed because God's Word has come and accomplished all that He intended for It—all that he purposed It. It has succeeded in that thing for which He sent it and these are the results.

Those who have been impacted by the Word of God go out in joy and are lead forth in peace. To be clear, that does not become like a Disney movie where they all live happily ever after. To the contrary adherence to the Word may bring forth more pain, sorrow, and difficulty. However, it brings the hearer joy and peace and grace and mercy that they have never experienced before. Nothing can compare to the penetrating mercy and grace of God's love. Nothing can even come close. Nothing can begin to change the heart of people like His Word does.

We, because of the wickedness in our hearts, try to let other things give us joy and peace. We think that any number of things that satisfy temporarily bring about true joy. We grab ahold of these things and allow them to consume our hearts. They become our idols. They become the objects of our worship. Our minds become convinced that our idols bring us joy.

Go to a local super market and walk up to the checkout line. Examine the covers of the magazines you find there. We are told that we can have the greatest and the best just by doing whatever it is that the people on the covers of those magazines are doing. We somehow believe that if we can look and act like them we will have something to delight in. If we have their lives, friends, and romantic relationships we will find happiness. We begin to think that if we have their homes, talent, and money we will have joy. However, what I see are people who *seem* to have it all while actually having little peace and joy. These are the people who seem to have arrived in life, have every possession you could ever want, and yet they have nothing that they can really hold on to.

The world promises a happiness and contentment that it cannot fulfill. If the world did not believe that these things could bring us happiness, it would not put them on these magazine covers because no one would buy them. I do not believe that the world is trying to sell us what they know to be a false premise. I truly think they believe that these things provide joy. To me it is reasonable to think that the person who writes these magazine articles about this or that celebrity believes that if he could have what the celebrity has, he would be happy.

The Word of God presents us with a different perspective. Joy, in Isaiah, is not tied to what we have. It is not connected to what we are. Joy is not dependent on where we are going in this life. The joy and peace that the Bible describes comes from God's Word accomplishing in us and around us exactly what He purposes It for. Just look at the results! The mountains and the hills break forth in singing. The trees are clapping their hands. There is joy when God revives.

Removing Weeds

Creation is excited about what God is doing with His Word. It is excited because God's work renews creation with His Word. He is renewing everything. His Word is right now causing the renewal of our fallen existence. Renewal is all around us. When His Word is at work, It takes dark, cold hearts, hardened by sin, and makes them into a heart of flesh (Ez 11:19, 26:26). His Word turns our hearts from hating God, His purpose, and His plan—from despising everything about Him—and turns our heart to our Heavenly Father. It makes our heart desire Him. His Word takes our heart from looking at ourselves and loving ourselves and our sin and It causes us to love Him.

He says in verse 12 that *instead of the thorn shall come up the cypress. Instead of the brier shall come up the myrtle*. The brier and the thorn are very undesirable. They are weeds that grow when things are left unattended—they grow up in unkept places.

Imagine two people who own houses beside each other. One of them has a yard that is well kept. They spend a lot of time and money taking care of it. They are really concerned about the appearance of their yard. They spend time grooming it. They invest time edging their driveway and sidewalks. They trim the bushes and hedges. They want to make sure it looks perfect.

Then you have the yard beside them. It is how my yard would look if I were responsible for the upkeep. It looks bad. It is unkept. No one cares whether or not there is edging work done. No one takes responsibility for the way the bushes and hedges grow. There is no attempt to keep weeds from mixing in with the grass. It is, frankly, an eye sore. No one seems to care about the yard. No one takes care of it. No one cares if it looks nice for those who pass by. There is no pride taken in the way the yard looks.

The Word of God is like the person with the yard who is well kept—the one who keeps things looking nice and always has. He leaves His yard and He goes to His neighbor. He goes to the one who does not care and has no desire to do better—the one who has no desire to make his yard look nice. This Neighbor leaves His home and visits the house beside Him. He knocks on the door and He offers to take care of the neighbor's yard. He offers to pull up the weeds—to pull up the briers. He offers to trim the bushes and hedges and make it look presentable. He does this with no expectation of pay and with the simple knowledge that He can help.

Planting Trees

When God plants His Word, the briers, the weeds, and the thorns are replaced. This stubble, that has no value and stands as a result of the yard not being tended to, disappears. After the briers and thorns are removed, the ground is not left as a barren wasteland. In fact, it is not even left as a neatly pruned yard. Something grows up in place of the undesirable plants. This passage draws my mind to Psalm 1. The psalmist speaks of a man who instead of walking in the counsel of the wicked, standing in the way of sinners, or sitting in the seat of scoffers, delights in the law of the Lord. The Law of the Lord is something he thinks about and mediates on day and night. The result of doing this, we are told, is that he becomes like a tree planted by streams of water. The tree yields its fruit in its season. The leaves of the tree do not wither and the man finds that he prospers in everything that he does.

This is much like the picture that we see in Isaiah 55. We see that the thorn and the brier are replaced with trees of value. They are replaced, not with something small or insignificant, but by something of worth. He makes the cypress tree come up in place of the thorn and the myrtle come up in place of the brier. Not only are these trees that are useful and lovely, but they are evergreen trees. They have long life spans and are desirable plants.

Unlike the brier and thorns that cause danger, these do nothing of the sort. God, when His Word comes, replaces the undesirable with strong trees—trees that He said in Psalm 1 are representative of the one who is in love with His Law (His Word).

Suddenly, these thorns and briers are replaced with great trees that are good and attractive. This is exactly what God intends to do to us. When He sends His Word into our hearts, it takes those neglected places that have been left in stubble and disrepair and He makes them new! He gives our lives value and worth. Our hearts are transformed by the falling rain and snow of His word. Our lives are turned into an offering to God that is lovely and presentable.

How great it is that He is willing to do that for us. God's Word revives nations and God's Word revives sinners. God's Word also revives each and every heart among His children. God's Word is planted in our hearts and is on our lips. When we dwell on It He sends us His great revival. I cannot escape the fact that God was willing, through His Son, to take my heart and pull out the weeds. He then planted something there for Himself. He planted the garden of His love in my heart.

I hope you have been able to see the passion with which our great God sends His Word. It is more than clear that we need His Word to guide us. Paul tells those gathered in Acts 17, that in Christ "we live and move and have our being" (v. 28). God has breathed out His Word and it completes us (2 Tim 3:16-17). When we fall in love with It—accept Its invitation, understand Its scope, rest on Its foundation, and enjoy Its results—God will revive us in ways we have never thought possible.

6

Discipline Yourself in the Word

Our next two chapters are for the practical application of our journey thus far. Mark Dever in *Nine Marks of a Healthy Church* writes, "The Word of God must be central to our lives and as a church because God's Spirit uses the Word to create faith in us and because He also uses the Word to make us grow" (p. 50). Our goal should be to constantly grow in our knowledge, understanding, and application of the Word.

There are eight areas that I want us to explore together. None of them are profound at all. However, being intentional in these eight disciplines has been beneficial for me in cultivating a love for God's Word. These are areas where God has revived my heart and life through their application. I pray that He will do so in your life as well. Four are listed in this chapter and involve disciplining ourselves to live in God's Word in our personal time. The next chapter will look at four areas where we live in God's Word within our community of faith.

Read the Word

The first area is probably the simplest of all: read the Word. Take time to read what God has said. I am always amazed at the number of people who claim to know what is said in God's Word and yet have seemingly never cracked it open. They are the type that would believe Hezekiah is a book in the Bible (it is not by the way). This person gives out wisdom in quotes that are supposedly from the sacred Scriptures. Yet a simple word search will not turn up what they claim is there. They simply neglect reading God's Word.

If we do not read It, then It will not renew our heart. We are blessed by the fact that God instructed men long ago to write down what He has said. Therefore, we should spend ample time reading it. In this area, I am talking about reading it without anything else complicating it. We should read it to enjoy what God has said. This is not reading with a commentary or study notes. We should simply read it to hear God speak and enjoy the fact that He has spoken to us. There is joy in the fact that our God is not silent, and we find it when we simply read. If you do not know where to start or you want to try a fresh approach to reading the Scriptures, let me suggest you pick up R.C. Sproul's *Knowing Scripture.* He has an excellent plan for reading the Bible thoroughly without getting bogged down.

Study the Word

Studying the Word takes our reading a step further. This *is* reading the Bible with a commentary in hand. We should utilize appropriate tools that have been given to us by godly people who have made themselves scholars of His Word. They have studied so that they would know what God has spoken. We should take time to study the Word.

We do this by taking small portions of the Word, reading them, and rereading them. We should look at the context of the passage and know the background of the passage. We then can dissect the text. We should mark keywords and phrases. It is helpful to take special note of things that are repeated over and over. We need to draw out and be aware of the various theological implications of the text. There are many portions of God's Word, if not all of God's Word, where a single verse could be studied for weeks and months and years and there would still be much to learn about from the passage.

I have a friend who has been studying the seventeenth chapter of John's Gospel for what seems to me like forever. I have heard him preach multiple messages from that chapter. He has taken the time to study the chapter from every perspective. He seems to know its flow, its implications, and theological significance of every word.

However, he would freely admit that there is still much more to learn. How exciting to think that we could be so in love with God's Word that we delve that deeply into what God is saying.

Study about the Word

In conjunction with the previous two disciplines, we should study about the Word. One thing that, for me, has made the Word more alive and powerful is studying about its composition—actually taking the time to know how the Bible was put together. This is an exercise in understanding the human author, the context in which he was writing, the context of his audience, and how the Word was transmitted to him from God. This may seem to some as only a pursuit to be undertaken by seminarians or Bible college students. It may be something that you have never put any thought into. If that is the case, my question is why? Why not know everything you can about God's Word? How can we make claims about the Word if we know nothing about It?

Every religious belief has some type of document that they claim as sacred. Each one of them has some collection of writings that they see as divine or at least divinely given. What separates the Word? What separates what God has said from what all the other religions of the world tell their followers? I do not believe it is sufficient to simply say "this is what God has said." I wholeheartedly believe that the

Bible is what God has said, but how do we know? How can we trust God's Word and know that It is reliable?

A study of the origins of the Bible and its composition will provide us information that we can compile, use, and study. To me, it is very clear that when we study about God's Word, we see His handiwork. We are able to see how He guided those who wrote to us, inspired what they said, and gave them the information necessary for us to know about Him.

This is a place where you want to find reliable sources to study because it is an academic discipline with many varied opinions. It is, however, quite possible to get ourselves through the noise and scholarly jargon and still come away better understanding God's Word. It is of no benefit for us to make claims about what God has said and done if we know little to nothing about the Word we so cherish.

Pray the Word

The final discipline I want to present in this chapter is praying the Scriptures. Prayer is the fuel of our spiritual journey. J. Chris Schofield writes, "The tendency in prayer is often to treat it as something we just do, making it like a ritual or a task. Prayer is relational and is something we 'are.' We cannot separate ourselves from our prayers. God answers his followers not just the prayer they pray" (v. 36).

This discipline will enrich your knowledge of God's Word and will cause you to grow more deeply in love with

It. This is exactly what it sounds like. In your prayer time—
in your conversations with God—open up your Bible and
pray from God's Word. Take a passage, maybe one that
you have been studying, and pray it back to God. We can
pray for the knowledge that He talks about, the hope that
He describes, or the gifts of grace and mercy that He has
spoken of. We can take passages where He has called us to
love our neighbor and pray to God for His help in loving
our neighbor. When we read passages about God's promise

of peace, that passage can be the foundation for our cry for peace. Let me give you a simple example from Psalm 23:

> *Lord, be my shepherd and keep me from wanting*
> *Make me lie down in green pastures of your abundance*
> *And lead me beside the still waters that calm my fears*
> *God, restore my broken and down cast soul.*
> *God, your path is righteous and if I am to carry your name*
> *I need you to lead me to protect it*
> *God, in life or in death*
> *I have no fear*
> *For you are with me*
> *And you comfort me with guidance and correction.*
> *I have victory over all enemies because of you.*
> *You have given me what I do not deserve*
> *And have given me more than I need*
> *In you, goodness and mercy shall follow me always*
> *And I know I will spend eternity with you.*
> *Amen*

This is not a formula to impress when you stand up to pray in public. Remember, Jesus was not a big fan of such prayers (Mt 6:7). It is, for me, a powerful way to keep our prayers focused on the priorities God has given us in His Word. Though this is simple, it is not really something we remember to do often. I am not sure if there is a better way to communicate with God than through His Word.

I have a particular friend who spends a great amount of time in prayer. In fact, it is His job—to pray and to help others to do so. He strives to help people in their prayer life. On a number of occasions I have heard Him speak of the great gift He has received in being able to encourage people to pray. When he does, he encourages people to make their prayers focus on the Father. When I stop and think about my prayer life, I realize that it very often revolves around me—what I want and hope for. I want God to do certain things for me. Often, I forget to talk about what God wants from me. The things that I want are temporal things that do not last. Many of my prayers have no impact on eternity. They have little value.

When we pray God's Word, we are praying the things that are on His heart. It is clear that they are there because He has given them to us in His Word—the revelation of His heart. I think it is interesting that people twist the Scriptures to say whatever they want by saying God will give us whatever we ask. We fail to see this statement is within the context of His will (1 Jn 5:14-15). Pleading for the will of God is the only prayer He always answers in the affirmative. His will is always done without exception. When we pray the Scriptures, we are praying from God's promises. They may sometimes be hard to understand and they often involve things that have not yet happened.

However, our God keeps His promises and we can find great security in praying the Scriptures.

We must also not forget that prayer is the place God gives us understanding for difficult passages in His Word. Spurgeon writes, in *Holy Spirit Power*, "Whenever you cannot understand a text, open your Bible, bend your knee, and pray over that text. If it does not splint into atoms and open itself, try again. If prayer does not explain it, it is one of the things God did not intend you to know, and you may be content to be ignorant of it" (p. 68). We need to have faith in God's movement in assisting us in understanding His Word.

7

Discipline Yourself in the Community of the Word

Our second chapter for disciplines of the Word will focus on four areas that revolve around living in the Word within the context of our community of faith. The Christian life is not one that is to be spent alone. We cannot be what we have been called in Christ to be and remain isolated from other Christians and their influence on our understanding of God's Word. If we are honest, it is often the influence of others that has molded and shaped us into who we are today.

It is very likely that you came to faith with one or more Christians around you, speaking into your life. Even those who come to faith in some private moment feel a strong sense to find other believers and share with them the good news of what Christ has done. These final three disciplines are intrinsically tied to both being influenced by other believers and reciprocating that influence onto new or potential Christian disciples.

Hear the Word Taught

As believers in Christ, we need to hear the Word taught. We do not come to the Bible knowing everything about it. In that moment when God saves us from our sin and delivers us from darkness He does not give us complete knowledge of all things—we do not have complete understanding of the Word of God. In fact, many spend their entire lives working toward a deeper knowledge of God's Word. There are those who do still come to the end of their life admitting that they do not know everything. Therefore, it is imperative that we who believe in Christ and cherish His Word hear the Word of God taught.

I do not believe it is sufficient to study God's Word on our own. I have spent a number of years in seminary and I have had multiple professors who know much more about God's Word than I. I attended class, read the textbook, took notes, and studied the information I was given. I came away understanding that there is a lot that I do not understand. However, I finished my time in seminary knowing much more about what God has said and who He is than when I started. That is the ultimate goal of exploring

God's Word. We want to come away knowing more about our Creator. When we do that, the rest falls in place.

We cannot gain this understanding on our own. While we are to study God's Word, we need to listen to teaching from people who are on this journey with us. They walk the same road we do, but many are further along than we are. They have spent more time on the journey and they have information about God's Word and who He is that is helpful for us.

We, as believers in Christ, are not on an island. This journey is not one we take alone. There are many pilgrims on the journey with us. John Hammett writes, "the Bible teaches and experience confirms that we are made for community. Yet all the manifestations of sin…frustrate our attempts to build community" (p. 398). We should spend whatever time is available to us learning from these fellow travelers. Again, some of them are going to be much further along than we are and have insight and knowledge that we will never gain on our own. If we simply try to take God's Word, decipher and understand it on our own, we will always come up short of what God has for us.

If we look throughout history, those who decide to become an island unto themselves do not fare well. They try to sit down and learn everything about God on their own outside of the community of faith. Those who do, often end up outside the orthodox doctrines of the church because there is no one there to help encourage them to stay within the bounds of God's Word. J. Gregory Lawson, in *Patterns of Discipleship in the New Testament as Evidenced by Jesus and Peter*, writes "The most effective way to combat the false teachers was to expose their evil deeds by the truth of God's Word. The false teachers spoke their own false words. Peter admonishes, 'No prophesy of Scripture comes from one's own interpretation' (2 Pet 1:20). It came instead as men were 'moved by the Holy Spirit, men spoke from God' (2 Pet 1:21). Divine inspiration, not human effort, provided the Scriptures. The Word of God becomes the best weapon for the disciple to face the false teachers. This is why it is absolutely essential for believers to grow in their understanding of the Word of God" (pp. 135-36).

All of this is traced back to the fact that we as believers live in a community of faith. We do not travel through life alone. As Ken Coley shows in the *Christian Education Journal*, the goal of Bible teaching "is to assists students by stimulating the construction of absolute truth with their mental framework and not the manifestation of a personal, relativistic truth" (p. 362). If we are placing ourselves under sound teaching, we will be greatly aided in knowing the truth.

Hear the Word Preached

I do not want you to confuse the previous section and this one. I believe hearing the Word preached and taught are two separate situations. When the Word is taught it is normally going to be done in some type of smaller situation. Teaching may be carried out through some type of correspondence or in a classroom setting in a Bible study with a pastor or Sunday school teacher. There are countless ways the Word of God can be taught.

When I think about the Word of God being preached, I am thinking about a different event. Preaching involves a preacher proclaiming "thus says the Lord." It is a situation involving someone as envisioned in 2 Timothy 4. Paul writes to Timothy, "I charge you in the presences of God and of Christ Jesus, who is to judge the living and the dead, and by his appearing and his kingdom: preach the word." He goes on to give him three (though certainly not the only) characteristics of preaching the Word—reprove, rebuke, exhort. William D. Mounce, in his excellent commentary on the Pastoral Epistles, shows why these three are so vital in pointing the believer in Christ toward a proper understanding of God's Word.

Reproving deals with the calling out of false teaching (p.574). As I have mentioned earlier, this is a problem that confronts us if we try to live out our Christian lives without being in the company and under the instruction of other believers. Paul gives this to Timothy as a primary task. A preacher who does not have this as part of his normal philosophy of preaching has failed to preach the Word. At the same time, if we do not submit ourselves to the reproving of a preacher, we are not taking advantage of the gift of correction that God makes available to us by godly preachers.

Rebuking is a strong word. It is used of Jesus' comments toward demons in the Gospels. While reproving is often hard for Christians to handle, rebuking has become almost unacceptable in the church. This is to be Timothy's reaction to those who refuse to listen when he reproves those who teach false doctrine. A preacher of God's Word has no option but to rebuke after listening to those who teach a false message and refuse to change when shown their error. The gospel is far too precious to allow it to be altered without a strong rebuke. If you are truly seeking to know God's Word and have It affect your life, you will seek after preaching that rebukes false teaching.

Finally, exhorting is encouragement "to live out the gospel in a life of righteousness" (p. 574). Timothy was to carry out the task of exhorting to encourage those who listened to his reproves and rebukes. The point of the Christian life is to live out the Gospel. Without being reminded of this, it is easy to fall into a false notion of what we have been called to do. We are not to simply believe the right things, but to actually live out what we have been called to do. A preacher of the Word will speak this truth into our lives.

The preacher is not given the command to preach his opinion or his thoughts. He is to preach the Word, calling people who are listening to the Word to a response. If we as believers in Christ do not have someone who is preaching the Word to us then we do not have someone who is calling on us to respond. This is the difference in preaching and teaching. Do not misunderstand that teaching, if done correctly, will cause a response in the learner. Preaching, however, is an action where a response is commanded.

We, as human beings, do not like to be told what to do—we also do not like being told there is a response necessary and being called on to respond. However, the fact is the Word demands a response. To that end, Sproul writes, "Many of us have become sensuous Christians, living by our feelings rather than through our understanding of the Word of God" (p. 31). We want to do it our way and with our timing. God does not praise the way of thinking.

Quite honestly, we will respond to God's Word one way or the other. We will either listen to the message of the preacher of God's Word by carrying out those things that God has called us to do or we will say "no." We will disobey. That is the choice that God places before us—the choice of life or death. We are given the choice to decide "this day whom we will serve" (Jo 24:15).

However, if we are not listening to the Word of God preached, we will not know that we need to respond. In turn, we will not be confronted at those times when we are failing to respond. Preaching, again going back to 2

Timothy 4, is an event that makes the hearer uncomfortable when he is not responding. While we are very content in our comfort, this is not where God would have us be. This is why He gives preachers who will proclaim and preach His Word so that the hearers will be called to a response. If we neglect to hear the Word preached, we will become very complacent, being satisfied with our current spiritual condition. In that condition, we will not respond as we would have if we had been sitting under the preaching of God's Word.

Discuss the Word

Next, I believe it is important to talk with other believers about the Word. I am the type that really likes having conversations with people. I was sitting the other day with a number of other pastors who were sharing humorous stories that they had experienced during their time in ministry. While many of these stories would not be funny to most listeners, they were beyond humorous to those of us sitting at the table because they were reflective of the common experience of ministry. I have learned much about the work of the ministry and the minister by talking with other pastors.

The same is true when it comes to God's Word. As I mentioned above, we live in a community of faith. We do not live and function on our own. God has called us to be a family—a body—therefore we must function as such. It is therefore natural for us to discuss the Word of God with other believers. Our conversations should be seasoned with discussions of the Word of God. This is a great way for us to keep our focus off of the things of this world—both the things which may be good and the things that cause us worry and stress. If we will talk about and think about the Word of God, we can avoid many of the pitfalls that so ensnare us. There are many things we can learn from one another simply in our discussions about what we are studying, what we have been reading, and how God is speaking to us through the Word.

This is not something we have to do in such a formal way as to seem awkward or off-putting to our fellow believers. It should, however, arise naturally. If it does not come naturally, we should make it intentional! Maybe you could start by selecting a friend who shares in your common love for the Word. Spend a time each week reading a verse or short passage together. When you spend time with your friend each week, discuss this passage. This does not have to be in some structured way where you are doing scholarly research on the passage. Just celebrate the joy of having been given that passage from God. Talk about the greatness of God as explained and exposed by the passage. Talk with your friend about how the passage has worked in your life during the week or how the passage is impacting other people around you. If there is joy found in God's Word, there is joy in talking about it.

There are countless ways you can discuss a passage of Scripture. Through this exercise, you will fall more and more in love with God's Word. You will end up sharing that love with others the more you spend time talking with other believers about God's Word.

This is an area that we do neglect. It is a lot simpler to talk with my friends about our mutual love for football or about things happening in my family. I can more easily talk about television shows than the Word. It is much more difficult to take the time to talk about what God's Word is doing to my heart and life. I hold God's Word precious but neglect to speak about it. It is difficult for me to understand why I do this. It may seem somewhat awkward to begin this discussion. However, let me make you this promise. If you start to have this type of relationship with other believers, not only will your love for God's Word deepen, but so will the love you have for your friends. They will see how God's Word is reviving your heart and your life and you will see God move in them.

Share the Word

We come to the eighth and final practical exercise for living in the Word. This section is probably the most difficult of the sections in our chapter. We explored, back in chapter three, that God desires to save sinners. It is the great news of the scope of His reviving power. He wants to infiltrate the hearts and minds of those who are deeply ensnared in sin and rescue them.

He has sent His Son who has died in our place. He desires that the news of His Son go out to all nations and all sinners. Therefore, it is necessary for us—we who believe in Christ and love His Word—to share the news of God's redemption with the world that is lost and dying. Sharing the Word is the natural reaction to our previously explored disciplines. The more we fall in love with God's Word, the more difficult it will be for us to keep that good news within our heart and mind. We will not be able to keep from sharing it with others.

One of the great commands that God gives us is to go. In Matthew 28:19, we are told to go and make disciples. He says in verse 19 to *Go and make disciples of all nations, baptizing them in the name of the Father, the Son and Holy Spirit.* He says to make disciples—replicate yourself, making people who are in love with God and His Word. Going on into verse 20, we are told to teach them to observe all that He has commanded. The question is then, where did He give us these commands? He did so through His Word. It is the things that He has spoken that He calls on us to teach people who do not know Him. We are to make disciples by sharing with them the Word.

When we do they can know the love and hope that is only found in Christ.

We are hard pressed to convince anyone that we love God and are His true disciples if we do not share the Word with others. This is something that we need to discipline ourselves to do. If we are not intentional about sharing the Word, I fear it will never become part of our natural routine of life. Larry S. McDonald writes, "At times evangelism streams from the natural overflow of a Christian's life. But it must be realized that evangelism does not take place only within the context of emotional motivation. Evangelism comes from a heart of obedience to Christ's command" (p. 153).

When we consider that the God of the universe has spoken to us and we have great hope in Him, it should become much easier for us to share His message with those who have not heard. They will never know of the great God who has spoken and therefore will never find delight in Him.

8

It Shall Not Return Void

As this book is coming to a close, we are reminded that God's Word tells us about a journey that we take in our relationship with God. As God's Word impacts our lives—falling upon us—It is renewing us. It is reviving us in a way that nothing else can. Nothing else that we can take into our lives, nothing else we have been invited to consume (Jer 15:16), can ever impact us the way God's Word will. The promise that God's Word will not return void is exciting and encouraging, but how does He accomplish it?

The Spirit and the Word

There is one common thing—a glue that holds them together. The eight things that we looked at in the previous two chapters should not be understood as an exhaustive list. There are plenty of others. Many other disciplines that believers have embraced throughout history have helped and prepared them to know and love God's Word. But what makes it work? Only one thing separates the believer in Christ who is reading God's Word and everyone else who simply picks up the Bible, reads it, and dismisses it as fantasy or fable. It is the indwelling of God's Holy Spirit.

Henry Blackaby and Claude King, in *Experiencing God*, write: "the Spirit uses the Word of God (the Sword of the Spirit—Eph. 6:17) to reveal God and His purpose. The Spirit uses the Word of God to instruct us in the ways of God" (p. 164). None of the things I have mentioned in the previous chapters will have any effect on you outside of the Spirit of God dwelling in your heart. The Spirit gives these disciplines their effectiveness—illuminating the Word for us so that we understand what God has said, has done, and desires for us.

In his *Institutes of Christian Religion*, John Calvin writes, "Enlightened by him (the Holy Spirit) we no longer have to rest on our own judgment or that of others, that the Scriptures are from God. Rather we can feel completely sure, in a way far above human opinion and just as though we could see God's picture stamped on them, that they came to us from the very mouth of God, using men as his instruments" (p. 43). Again, God does not leave us alone to try to figure out what He has said. He has not only given us His Word, but He gave us His Spirit as the "Great Interpreter." As you begin to put into place disciplines necessary to know and love God's Word, do not stray far from the teaching of the Spirit. Calvin makes it clear that the Spirit is the guide and defender of the Scriptures. He is able to convince even the most hardened skeptic of the reliability and power of God's Word (pp. 41-45).

Paul, as he wrote to hurting churches and Christians, declared that it was only through the power of the Holy Spirit that a person could claim Jesus as Lord (1 Cor 12:3). He writes elsewhere that, "Our gospel came to you not only in word, but also in power and in the Holy Spirit and with full conviction" (1 Thess 1:5). The Holy Spirit is God's confirmation of His Word and Its power! The writer of Hebrews goes as far as to make the clear connection that it is the Holy Spirit that has inspired the biblical writers to pen the words that God provided (Heb 3:7). As you take this journey in God's Word, rejoice that He has placed His Spirit in you. You do not travel alone and you need only to let His Spirit guide you through His Word.

As You Travel

I think about some of the guys I would call my best friends. In a previous community where I pastored, I had three friends who were ministers in other churches. We spent a lot of time together. Though some of us have moved on to different places of ministry, we still remain in contact. In many ways we were an odd group. We were very different people. We carried out our ministries differently. We had different views about our roles in ministry and what things we should be doing in ministering to the people of our churches. We had different theological ideas. Some of those ideas we would strongly debate among ourselves. These debates were often lively and fun.

However, there was always one thing that we came back to regardless of our disagreements and thoughts. We came back to the common love that we shared for the Word of God. It is really the thing that brought us together in the first place. Honestly, I would say that our love for the Word of God served more as a reason for our friendship than our common occupation. We loved God's Word so much that we felt we had to preach and proclaim It. God's Word was what drove us.

Now having moved from that community, the loss of that bond is what I miss most. We no longer have that opportunity to share with one another about our common love for God's Word. That is the affect that God's Word has. It is a bond that binds believers with Christ and one another. When it is absent, it is sorely missed.

The Word is a story. Not the story of us, what we have done, what we accomplished, or where we are going. That would make it a mere book of history, sociology, or psychology. The Word is the story of God, who He is, what He has done, and where He is taking all things. Within that context we can learn about ourselves—we can learn who we are. God's story is about His love for His people. It tells of our fall, our salvation, and about our eternal destiny. However, it is primarily about God and His character. It reveals to us that He loves sinners and has an unquenchable thirst to redeem them from the bondage of sin. We are told of the Christ on His undeterrable mission to purchase redemption with His blood. We read of His passionate pursuit of those who He would transfer from the domain of darkness to His glorious light (Col 1:13).

It tells us about a God who, in the beginning, not because He was lonely or bored, but because He is good and creative, spoke out of eternity and made everything that is. We are told the story of God who, when His creation disobeyed Him, doing the one thing they were told not to do, He still showed them love. He covered their nakedness and did not kill them in that moment but gave them the opportunity to turn from their sin and return to fellowship with Him.

The Word tells us about God's constant and persistent pursuit of His people. When they were in a faraway land, He called a man out of that land and promised Him that he would be the father of a great nation. When His people were captive in slavery, He promised they would be delivered and He kept that promise. When they wanted a king, though they had the eternal King, He gave them a man who occupied a throne that He promised would never end. Even then, with a great king, the story remained about God.

He spoke through prophets, who delivered His Word to the people. We read of instance after instance where the Word of God came to the prophets. The Word of God came to Jonah (Jon 1:1). The Word of God came to Zephaniah (Zep 1:1). The Word of God came to Hosea (Hos 1:1). To each of these the Word of God came and He spoke to the people. We are privileged to be left with a record of what He said. He does not want us to be ignorant or to go through life with no idea about what He wants, thinks, or calls us to do.

God gives us His Word and after hundreds of years of silence, a man appears in the wilderness. He is a strange looking man. He eats strange food and proclaims a strange message. Despite this, he speaks the Word of God. He proclaims that there is One coming that is greater than he. One who will baptize, not with water, but with the Holy Spirit and fire. There was One coming and the Word of God tells us His story—the story of the Prince of Peace. This is the most important story of all. We are privileged enough to hear the story of the High Priest who dies on our behalf. He is the One who is King, Prophet, Priest, and Sacrifice. He is the propitiation who causes God to look favorably on the sinners who had betrayed Him. Now sinners have the opportunity to know their God and walk with the Prince of Peace.

He tells us of His Son who goes to a cross and dies. His Son, who committed no wrongs and knew no sin, became sin for us (2 Cor 5:21). That same Son, who after walking in obedience to His Father, dies in that same obedience. He tells us in Hebrews 5, we should obey as well. Through obedience to the Father, He won salvation full and free. His salvation is enjoyed by all who obey—to all who believe and repent of their sins, turning to Him. What a powerful story!

His story tells us there is an end point coming. There is a day when His Son will return and He will call home His children. Everything that has been messed up since Genesis 3 when first His people turned from His Word will come to an end. He will no longer speak the way He has before. There will no longer be a need to read His Word, because all of creation will see Him as He is—we will see the Word. All the earth will witness the risen Christ and the glory of the Father.

This is the story. This is the Word of God. Why would we neglect such a great salvation? Why would be neglect to read and digest and consume and fall in love with His Word?

John Newton, the 18th century pastor and author of the hymn "Amazing Grace," writes in his autobiography about his spiritual journey from slave trader to pastor. When, after years of his mother's prayers, he finally is saved by Christ, he writes about his insatiable need to consume the Scriptures. He learns the biblical languages and gives up his study of classical literature and mathematics. He writes that, "I have given myself chiefly to writing and have not found time to read many books besides the Scriptures" (p. 123).

Before Newton died, he had penned the epitaph that still hangs at St. Mary Woolnoth in London where he was the pastor. He wrote that he was "once an infidel and libertine. A servant of slaves in Africa. Was, by the rich mercy of our Lord and Saviour Jesus Christ, reserved, restored, pardoned, and appointed to preach the faith he had long labored to destroy" (p. 158). The Word conquered the dark heart of this slave trafficker and made him into something beautiful.

We need to be revived. We must seek it afresh each morning. We need hope and help in times of our struggle. God has provided it to us in His Word. He wants us to be madly in love with His Word and consume it. We must do this because it shall not return void.

BIBLIOGRAPHY

Akin, Daniel L. *Five Who Changed the World.* Wake Forest: Southeastern Baptist Theological Seminary, 2008.

Blackaby, Henry T., and Claude V. King. *Experiencing God.* Nashville: Broadman & Holman Publishers, 1994.

Calvin, John. *Calvin's Commentary.* Vol. VIII. XXII vols. Grand Rapids: Baker Books, 1984.

—. *The Institutes of the Christian Religion.* Edited by Tony Lane and Hilary Osborne. Grand Rapids, MI: Baker Academic, 1987.

Carson, D.A. *A Call to Spiritual Reformation.* Grand Rapids: Baker Academic, 1992.

Coley, Kenneth S. "Active Learning Techniques in the Christian Education Classroom and Ministry Contexts." *Christian Education Journal*, 2012: 357-371.

Dever, Mark. *9 Marks of a Healthy Church.* Wheaton: Crossway, 2004.

Dockery, David S., and David P. Nelson. "Special Revelation." In *A Theology for the Church*, by Daniel L. Akin, 118-174. Nashville: B&H Publishing Group, 2007.

Edwards, Jonathan. *Sermons of Jonathan Edwards.* Peabody: Hendrickson Publishers, 2005.

Hammett, John S. "Human Nature." In *A Theology for the Church*, by Daniel L. Akin, 340-408. Nashville: B&H Publishing Group, 2007.

Lawson, James Gregory. "Patterns of discipleship in the new
    testament as evidenced by Jesus and Peter."
    Southwestern Baptist Theological Seminary, 2013.

Lloyd-Jones, Martyn. *Revival.* Wheaton: Crossway, 1987.

McDonald, Larry Steven. "Myths Surrounding the "Gift of
    Evangelism"." In *A Passion for the Great Commission:
    Essays in Honor of Alvin L. Reid*, edited by Larry Steven
    McDonald and Matt Queen, 141-156. Greer, SC:
    Towering Oaks Books, 2013.

Mohler, Jr., R. Albert. *Words from the Fire.* Chicago: Moody
    Publishers, 2009.

Mounce, William D. *Word Biblical Commentary: Pastoral
    Epistles.* Edited by Bruce M. Metzger, Ralph P. Martin
    and Lynn Allan Losie. Vol. 46. 52 vols. Nashville, TN:
    Thomas Nelson, 2000.

Newton, John. *Out of the Depths.* Grand Rapids: Kregel
    Publications, 2003.

Norman, R. Stanton. "Human Sinfulness." In *A Theology for the
    Church*, by Daniel L. Akin, 480-544. Nashville: B&H
    Publishing Group, 2007.

Pink, Arthur W. *Spiritual Growth.* Grand Rapids: Baker Books,
    1971.

Piper, John. *Desiring God.* Colorado Springs, CO: Multnomah,
    2003.

Roberts, Richard Owen. *Repentance: The First Word of the
    Gospel.* Wheaton: Crossway, 2002.

Schofield, J. Chris. "Missional Prayer Patterns From John 17 with Application for Spiritual Awakening." In *A Passion for the Great Commission: Essays in Honor of Alvin L. Reid*, edited by Larry Steven McDonald and Matt Queen, 33-46. Greer, SC: Towering Oaks Books, 2013.

Shaeffer, Francis A. *He is there and he is not silent.* Wheaton: Tyndale House Publishing, 1972.

Sproul, R.C. *Knowing Scripture.* Downers Grove: InterVarsity Press, 2009.

Spurgeon, Charles Haddon. *Holy Spirit Power.* New Kensington: Witaker House, 1996.

—. *Spurgeon's Sermon Notes.* Peabody: Hendrickson Publishers, 1997.

ABOUT THE AUTHOR

Micheal S. Pardue, Sr. serves as the Pastor of First Baptist Church Icard, NC and has served five other churches in the Foothills of North Carolina. Micheal holds a Master of Christian Ministry from the T. Walter Brashier Graduate School at North Greenville University and a Doctorate of Education from Southeastern Baptist Theological Seminary.

Dr. Pardue has had the privilege of speaking in more than numerous churches, colleges, and Baptist associations across the United States and Internationally. He has previously served on the Executive Committee of the Baptist State Convention of North Carolina and as President of the North Carolina Pastors' Conference. He currently serves the BSCNC as First Vice President.

He and his wife, Rachel, have seven children. For more information about Micheal, his ministry, and his writing go to www.michealpardue.com or follow him on Twitter @michealpardue.

STUDY GUIDE

This study guide is designed to give your group the most flexibility as you read *It Shall Not Return Void.* The guide offers guided discussion activities that are designed to encourage conversation and participation. Please encourage your group to make notes in the book as the read so that they are prepared to participate each time you meet. The guide for each chapter is broken down into these four sections:

Prepping the Meal: This section provides some initial discussion starters that can be completed with a partner or in a smaller sub-group. This section allows the members of the group to share some highlights from their reading and is designed to get the group thinking about the implications of the chapter they have read and begin to apply it to their life.

Eat this Book!: This section will look at the Scripture passage discussed in the chapter or one relevant to the topic. Encourage your students to read this passage and spend a few minutes discussing it as a group. A brief summary is provided to show how it connects with the chapter of *It Shall Not Return Void.* There are three statements or questions listed in bold. Have the group discuss all three with their partner/sub-group. Discuss the third as a large group.

Food for Thought: This section has the meat of the
discussion and encourages the group to dig deeper in
thinking about the implications of the book. Open ended
questions and discussion topics allow the group to develop
a further understanding of being revived in God's Word.

What's for Dessert?: This final section transitions the
group into thinking about what is ahead. This provides
the group a chance to briefly discuss what they will take
away from their time together and will allow them to pray
together before departing. This section also serves as a
preview of the next chapter and helps group members
focus in on what they are about to read.

Chapter 1

Prepping the Meal

Have the group breakup into smaller groups. With their group, have them brainstorm ideas in response to the question: **What would you say are the top five characteristics of revival?**

Call on groups to give their list and record the answers where the group can see. Discuss what the list says about our understanding of revival

Eat this Book!

Read: Psalm 85:1-7

The Psalmist desires to be revived. He knows that God has restored prior generations and his hope, in this psalm, is that God will revive his generation as well.

Name some times that God was angry with His people in the Old Testament:

What do you think it means to be restored by God?

What does this psalm tell us about how God revives His people?

Food for Thought

Have the group share some excerpts from the reading in chapter one that they found meaningful.

Why do you think it is so easy to believe that the spiritual condition of our culture is unique to our time?

God's Word is light in the darkness, rain in the desert, shelter for the homeless, asylum for the refugee, and hope for sinners. Respond to this statement from chapter one. Share with the group a time when you have seen God's Word work in this manner.

Why do you think it is so easy to believe that a simple change in someone's actions is a sign of revival?

What's for Dessert?

With their partner, have the group answer this: **In light of this chapter, what is one thing you can commit to changing this week?**

Once they have shared, encourage them to spend several minutes in prayer together asking God to work in their lives in light of this chapter and prepare them for your next gathering.

The next several chapters explore Isaiah 55. Charles Spurgeon called Isaiah 55 "the great chapter of gospel invitation." Make sure to keep this in mind as you explore Isaiah's words and this book.

Chapter 2

Prepping the Meal

Have the group breakup into smaller groups. With their group, have them brainstorm ideas in response to the question: **What are some areas in life where people often settle for less than the best?**

Call on groups to give their list and record the answers where the group can see. Picking several of their answers, ask the group why they think it is so easy to settle for less than the best.

Eat this Book!

Read: Isaiah 55:1-3

Isaiah gives God's invitation. This is an invitation to listen to the good news of God's reviving offer. God's offer is not merely food or drink. It is the invitation to an everlasting covenant.

What things does God invite people to in this passage?

According to this passage, what happens when you listen to God?

Why do you think that God links His revival with listening?

Food for Thought

Have the group share some excerpts from the reading in chapter two that they found meaningful.

Think of God's command to listen to Christ. **What is it about listening that is so difficult for human beings?**

If we think an event will cause revival to happen or if we think that our increased church attendance will cause God to send His blessings, we are sadly mistaken. Respond to this statement from chapter two. Ask the group **why it is so easy to trust in our own efforts instead of letting God work?**

When was a time when you exchanged God's bread
for something stale and moldy?

What are some of the things that you spend your
time and money on that have no benefit?

What's for Dessert?

With their partner, have the group answer this: **In light
of this chapter, what is one thing you can commit to
changing this week?**

Once they have shared, encourage them to spend several
minutes in prayer together asking God to work in their
lives in light of this chapter and prepare them for your
next gathering.

The next chapter looks at God's scope of revival. How big do you think God's revival is? As you read the next chapter, consider the areas that are explored that you had not thought about. If you did not consider how big God's revival is, does it limit you from being a part of His revival?

Chapter 3

Prepping the Meal

Have the group breakup into smaller groups. With their group, have them brainstorm ideas in response to the question: **What things cause us to have a narrow view of God's word?**

Call on groups to give their list and record the answers where the group can see. Picking several of their answers, ask the group why many people do not have a big enough view of God's revival.

Eat this Book!

Read: Isaiah 55:4-9

Something mysterious is happening here. Because of the Lord's word, a nation shall run to them that they did not know. God wants to do something here that is far greater than His dealings with one nation. It is time for revival to take place. The wicked should forsake his way, the unrighteous man his thoughts. The Lord is ready to forgive and pardon.

According to verse 5, why will the nations run to the people of God?

What action words does Isaiah use in verses 6 and 7 to call people back to their God?

What are some of the statements made in this passage that give you hope?

Food for Thought

Have the group share some excerpts from the reading in chapter three that they found meaningful.

After reading this chapter, what is God's scope of revival?

That God's renewal is for all nations is made clear in multiple Scripture passages....Throughout the biblical storyline, God seeks out the nations for salvation. Respond to this statement from chapter three. Ask the group what they think when they read these passages that describe people from every tribe and tongue and people and nation.

What are you doing to take part in the revival of the nations?

Why is God's promise to renew the nations hard for Christians to believe?

When was a time you were thankful that His ways were not your ways? Why?

What's for Dessert?

With their partner, have the group answer this: **In light of this chapter, what is one thing you can commit to changing this week?**

Once they have shared, encourage them to spend several minutes in prayer together asking God to work in their

lives in light of this chapter and prepare them for your next gathering.

The next chapter looks at God's foundation of revival. Picture the last time you witnessed a big snowfall. What did you think? Did you dread the work and inconvenience it might require or were you able to enjoy the beauty? As you read the next chapter, consider the comparison of snowfall to God's revival.

Chapter 4

Prepping the Meal

Have the group breakup into smaller groups. With their group, have them brainstorm ideas in response to these two questions: **What is your favorite place to eat? Where do you eat most often?**

Call on groups to give their list and record the answers where the group can see. Comparing the two lists, ask the group to discuss why they might have two different answers.

Eat this Book!

Read: Isaiah 55:10-11

This passage paints a beautiful picture of God's revival and renewal. He is at work in all phases. From beginning to end, He is guiding everything that happens. His picture of rain and snow transitions to the wonderful blessing of His Word. He promises that it will not return void.

What things do the rain and snow produce?

According to this passage, where does God's Word come from?

What do you believe God's Word seeks to accomplish and succeed in doing?

Food for Thought

Have the group share some excerpts from the reading in chapter two that they found meaningful.

After reading this chapter, **where is God's source of revival? Why?**

All of this is not random. It does not happen by chance—God does not just get lucky. He has a purpose in everything He does. Just as the rain and snow are indispensable, so is His Word. Nothing is accomplished without it. Respond to this statement from chapter four. Ask the group what they think when they read this excerpt and think about the vital nature of God's Word to their renewal.

How do you allow God's Word to renew you?

Why do you think it is so difficult to rely on God's Word for renewal?

How have you seen God's Word accomplish His purposes in your life?

What's for Dessert?

With their partner, have the group answer this: **In light of this chapter, what is one thing you can commit to changing this week?**

Once they have shared, encourage them to spend several minutes in prayer together asking God to work in their

lives in light of this chapter and prepare them for your next gathering.

The next chapter looks at the results of God's reviving Word. As you read the chapter, think about the results of God's Word penetrating your life. How has It changed you? Has It sufficiently changed you or is there still much to be done?

Chapter 5

Prepping the Meal

Have the group breakup into smaller groups. With their group, have them brainstorm ideas in response to the question: **What is your single greatest accomplishment and what was its effect on your life?**

Call on groups to give their list and record the answers where the group can see. Picking several of their answers, ask the group to talk about how they achieved this. **Was it on their own or with help?**

Eat this Book!

Read: Isaiah 55:12-13

The scene seems strange indeed. Mountains are singing and trees are clapping their hands. However, it is a scene of joy in the reviving power of God's Word. Because it does not return void, there is joy in the completion of Its work.

In verse 12, what leads a person when they experience the reviving power of God's Word? What is the difference between the briers and thorns and the myrtles and cypresses that come in their place?

Why do you think Isaiah describes how God's Word causes one thing to be replaced with another?

Food for Thought

Have the group share some excerpts from the reading in chapter two that they found meaningful.

After reading this chapter, what might it look like to be led forth in God's peace?

Those who have been impacted by the Word of God go out in joy and are lead forth in peace. To be clear, that does not become like a Disney movie where they all live happily ever after. To the contrary adherence to the Word may bring forth more pain, sorrow, and difficulty. However, it brings the hearer joy and peace and grace and mercy that they have never experienced before. Respond to this statement from chapter five. Ask the group what they think when they read that God's revival could bring forth pain, sorrow, and difficulty. **Why do they think this could happen?**

How do you think a person builds a foundation for God to renew them with His Word?

What's for Dessert?

With their partner, have the group answer this: **In light of this chapter, what is one thing you can commit to changing this week?**

Once they have shared, encourage them to spend several minutes in prayer together asking God to work in their lives in light of this chapter and prepare them for your next gathering.

The next chapter begins our look at some practical steps that you can take to develop your deep and abiding love for God's Word. As you read the chapter ahead, think about what God has used to develop your love for His Word. How can that be developed further?

Chapter 6

Prepping the Meal

Have the group breakup into smaller groups. With their group, have them brainstorm ideas in response to the question: **What are some things that should be simple but give you a lot of trouble?**

Call on groups to give their list and record the answers where the group can see. Picking several of their answers, ask the group why these things prove to be difficult.

Eat this Book!

Read: Joshua 1:6-9

Upon Moses' death, Joshua was chosen by God as the leader of His people. This was a daunting task, for sure, but it seems fitting that God would choose one of the two men who remained faithful when the crowd was afraid to lead His people. With the Promised Land ahead of them, God reminds Joshua how to find success.

What is Joshua told to do multiple times in this passage?

How often is Joshua to think about the things God has said?

Why do you think that God connects Joshua's knowledge of and obedience to His Word with success?

Food for Thought

Have the group share some excerpts from the reading in chapter six that they found meaningful.

After reading this chapter, which one of the *Discipline Yourself in the Word* disciplines are hardest for you? Why?

A study of the origins of the Bible and its composition will provide us information that we can compile, use, and study. To me, it is very clear that when we study about God's Word, we see His handiwork. Respond to this statement from chapter six. Ask the group what they think is important to know about God's Word. **Why might people be cautious to learn about God's Word?**

What things keep you from reading the word? Studying the Word? Studying about the Word? Praying the Word?

What's for Dessert?

With their partner, have the group answer this: **In light of this chapter, what is one thing you can commit to changing this week?**

Once they have shared, encourage them to spend several minutes in prayer together asking God to work in their lives in light of this chapter and prepare them for your next gathering.

The next chapter lists some of the ways we can discipline ourselves to live in the Word within the context of our Christian community. As you read the chapter ahead, think about what God has used to develop your love for His Word. How can that be developed further?

Chapter 7

Prepping the Meal

Have the group breakup into smaller groups. With their group, have them brainstorm ideas in response to the question: **What are your top three favorite things to do with a group of people?**

Call on groups to give their list and record the answers where the group can see. Picking several of their answers, ask the group if those things would be as much fun if done alone.

Eat this Book!

Read: 2 Timothy 3:14-17

In 2 Timothy, Paul warned Timothy that the Christian life would not be easy. As a Christian leader, he will experience resistance and hardship and will be constantly tempted to stray away from the truth of God. In teaching his young protégé how to resist temptation, Paul encouraged Timothy to remember what he had been taught and to live in the Word.

According to verse 15, the sacred writings are able to what?

According to verse 16, what four things are the Scriptures useful for?

What do you think it means to be complete and equipped for every good work?

Food for Thought

Have the group share some excerpts from the reading in chapter seven that they found meaningful.

After reading this chapter, which one of the *Discipline Yourself in the Community of the Word* disciplines are hardest for you? Why?

We, as believers, are not on an island. This journey is not one we take alone. There are many pilgrims on the journey with us. Respond to this statement from chapter seven. Ask the group what they think when they read this excerpt. **Why is it that some people try to live the Christian life alone?**

Why do you think that God intends for so much of our Christian life to be spent with others?

What things keep you from hearing the Word taught? Hearing the Word preached? Discussing the Word? Sharing the Word?

What's for Dessert?

With their partner, have the group answer this: **In light of this chapter, what is one thing you can commit to changing this week?**

Once they have shared, encourage them to spend several minutes in prayer together asking God to work in their lives in light of this chapter and prepare them for your next gathering.

Our final chapter sums up all we have learned about the reviving work of God's Word. The Spirit of God is our great gift that illuminates God's Word. He helps us to know and understand what God has said. As you read, consider the awesome gift we have been given because God has spoken to us.

Chapter 8

Prepping the Meal

Have the group breakup into smaller groups. With their group, have them brainstorm ideas in response to the question: **What do you feel is your biggest challenge to being revived?**

Call on groups to give their list and record the answers where the group can see. Picking several of their answers, ask the group what things that have learned during the study that can help them to overcome these challenges.

Eat this Book!

Read: 1 Corinthians 15:1-8

As Paul wraps up his first letter to the church at Corinth, he reminds them of many of the specifics of the gospel. He makes it clear that everything that happened was in fulfillment of the Scriptures. These are the things of first importance.

What does Paul say in verse one and two that allows them to stand and be saved?

How many people does Paul say saw Christ alive?

Why do you think it was important to remind them of the message of the Gospel?

Food for Thought

Have the group share some excerpts from the reading in chapter eight that they found meaningful.

After reading this chapter, what role does the Spirit play in your love of the Word?

We are told of the Christ on His undeterrable mission to purchase redemption with His blood. We read of His passionate pursuit of those who He would transfer from the domain of darkness to His glorious light (Co 1:13). Respond to this statement from chapter eight. Ask the group what they think when they read that God's Word tells the story of a God in pursuit of His people.

After reading about John Newton's deliverance from darkness, discuss how God has brought your out of darkness.

As we wrap up this study, how do you plan to strive to be revived in God's Word?

What's for Dessert?

With their partner, have the group answer this: **In light of this chapter, what is one thing you can commit to changing this week?**

Once they have shared, encourage them to spend several minutes in prayer together asking God to work in their

lives in light of this chapter and prepare them for what is ahead after the group is finished.